LET'S INVESTIGATE ART

CONFLICT IN ART

Clare Gogerty

Marshall Cavendish
New York • London • Toronto • Sydney

Published by
Benchmark Books
Marshall Cavendish Corporation
99 White Plains Road
Tarrytown, NY 10591

© Marshall Cavendish Corporation, 1997
© Cherrytree Press Ltd, 1996

Designed and produced by Touchstone Publishing Ltd

Cover: *Battle of Agincourt, 1415,* from St Alban's Chronicle

Picture acknowledgements: see page 47

Library of Congress Cataloging-in-Publication Data

Gogerty, Clare
    Conflict in art / Clare Gogerty.
        p. cm. — (Let's investigate art)
    Includes index.
    Summary: Examines the depiction of conflict and war in the art of various cultures throughout history. Also includes instructions for related projects and brief biographies of the artists mentioned in the text.
        ISBN 0-7614-0011-7 (library binding)
        1. War in art—Juvenile literature. 2. Art appreciation—Juvenile literature. [1. War in art. 2. Art appreciation.] I. Title. II. Series.
    N8260.G65 1996   96-4412
    704.9'4936902—dc20   CIP
                                                        AC

Printed and bound in Italy

Contents

In every chapter of this book you will find a number of colored panels. Each one has a symbol at the top to tell you what type of panel it is.

Activity panel Ideas for projects that will give you an insight into the techniques of the artists in this book. Try your hand at painting, sculpting and crafts.

Information panel Detailed explanations of particular aspects of the text, or in-depth information on an artist or work of art.

Look and See panel Suggestions for some close observation, using this book, the library, art galleries, and the art and architecture in your area.

Conflicts of old

Human beings, unfortunately, do not always live in harmony with one another. Conflict is continually present at home, at school, in the workplace and in the wider world. People's interests conflict and so do those of nationalities and nations. Somewhere, in some part of the world, there is a war. Somewhere, in every street, there is a quarrel. Conflict has always been part of our lives. Art reflects life, so conflict has often been the artist's subject.

Heroes for all time

From ancient times, soldiers have been honored and glorified and have been celebrated in art. In ancient Greece, the stories of mythical heroes were passed from generation to generation by word of mouth. The Greeks were often at war. Tales of their wars and warriors, real and mythical, inspired young men to become warriors and fight in battle. Their deeds of valor were recorded by artists in pictures on pots, in

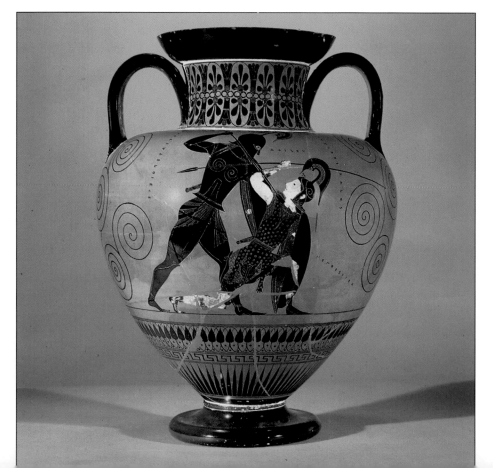

◄ *The scene on this amphora comes from the story of the Trojan war. It shows the Greek hero Achilles about to kill the queen of the Amazons (fierce female warriors who fought on the side of the Trojans). See how strong and clear the outlines are. Notice how the heads are in profile, even though the bodies are facing the front. Notice also the tension between the two figures, and how the artist has filled the spaces between them with patterns.*
[Athenian black-figured neck amphora, Athens, Exekias]

carvings and sculptures on public buildings and on the tombs where the warriors were buried.

Wealthy Greeks kept their wine and oil in two-handled pots called amphorae. These

they decorated with scenes from war, scenes that showed the glamour and glory of war – and none of its horrors.

The might of the Romans

The Romans were even more famous as soldiers than the Greeks. Their legions conquered most of the known western world, and their conquests brought them great wealth. They were also fine engineers. They used their skills and their wealth to construct grand public buildings, triumphal arches and columns. In elaborate carvings on these, they told the stories of their triumphs

▲ ▶ *These Roman mosaics show two figures from Greek myth. The figure above is Meleager, a proud warrior. The mosaic on the right shows his lover, Atalanta, the huntress. They look three-dimensional because the artist has used different tones of the same color, creating light, shade and an illusion of solidity.*

◄ *Although this is a gruesome scene (several people have lost their heads!), the overall impression is exuberant. This is because the artist has concentrated on decorating the page with pattern and color rather than making the scene realistic. Notice how the figures in the distance are the same size as those in the foreground. Perspective (see page 12) had not yet been invented. [An illustration from Abu'l-Qasim Firdawsi's* Shahnama *(Book of Kings)]*

and proclaimed in pictures the greatness of Rome. In their grand houses, the Romans laid mosaic floors, made of thousands and thousands of tiny rectangular pieces of stone and glass, carefully positioned to make patterns and pictures. The subjects of these pictures often included military triumphs or famous fighters.

The Persians

The ancient Persian kings were often at war with the Greeks and the Romans. Their victories were later recorded in beautiful handwritten books. The art of beautiful handwriting is called calligraphy. It became especially important in the Middle East in the 7th century when the people there were converted to Islam. The new religion forbade artists to depict living things, so in Islamic art and architecture there are few human beings or living animals. Instead there are elaborate and intricate patterns of great richness, and exquisite calligraphy.

One book that does contain images of people is the *Shahnama*, which means the Book of Kings. It was written by the poet Abu'l-Qasim Firdawsi during the 11th century AD and tells the troubled, bloodthirsty history of Persia (later Iran). The book is colorful and attractive despite its gory content. The people and horses look like cardboard cutouts, not like real warriors in battle.

Firing lines

Clay is transformed into pottery, like the Greek amphora on page 4, by firing (heating) it in a type of oven, called a kiln, to make it hard. To make the pottery waterproof and smooth, rather than porous and rough, it is painted with a coating called a glaze before firing. The Greeks painted stories on their pots.

Modern pottery is also often decorated. Look at the dishes, plates and pots in your home. Are they decorated with stories? Do any show conflicts? If not, what kinds of designs do they have? Look at pots in museums and in books. How has the shape of the crockery influenced the decoration?

The terracotta army

Emperor Qin Shi Huang Di of China was a ruthless tyrant. He persecuted his opponents and put to death those who tried to resist him. He sent armies out to extend China's territory and cruelly oppressed those he conquered. His power rested in his control of his army. He gave orders that when he died an "army" was to be buried with him, to impress all he met in the afterlife. The army was to consist of over 8,000 life-sized statues of warriors, some on horses, who would protect him in death as his living soldiers had protected him in life.

Craftsmen made the figures from terracotta, a brownish-red baked clay. They used molds for the bodies, but every head and pair of hands was individually carved so that each soldier had different features. The work must have taken years. For centuries the grim but superb statues stood guard, waiting for action. They remained buried until 1974, when the emperor's tomb was discovered by local villagers digging a well and was then unearthed by archaeologists.

Mosaic warriors

For their mosaics, the Romans used marble and other stones, glass and even shells. They set the pieces, called tesserae, into a bed of mortar (a mixture of cement and lime). You can make mosaics using pieces of gummed paper.

What you need
- gummed sheets of colored paper or magazine pictures
- water or glue • piece of card
- scissors • pencil

What you do
1 Imagine two people fighting. They can be warriors from ancient times, from today, or from the future.
2 Draw your warriors on to the card. Make the drawing simple and bold, and avoid too much detail. Concentrate on the shape of the heads and the way the figures are standing.
3 Cut the colored paper into squares and rectangles of varying sizes. You will need lots and lots of them.
4 Stick your "tesserae" on to the pencil outline. Look at the Roman mosaic on page 5. Notice how few colors the artist has used and how he has emphasized the eyes and horses' manes by outlining them in black. See if you can match his skill.
Note Instead of gummed paper, you could use pages torn from magazines and glue. The much greater range of colors will help you to achieve more subtle and lifelike effects.

The glory of war

Have you ever seen a film of a great medieval battle, with thousands of combatants in gleaming armor, charging into the fray, colorful banners flying? A scene like this does not tell us what war is really like because it hides from us the pain and suffering of the wounded. It shows only the excitement and glory of the fight.

Some paintings portray wars in the same way. The artist deliberately sets out to make the scene more heroic than it actually was.

Triumph of the imagination

The enormous scale and detail of some war paintings, such as the one by Albrecht Altdorfer (opposite), is breathtaking. Altdorfer had not witnessed the battle himself – it took place centuries before he was born. He read accounts of the battle to find out how many soldiers fought and what sort of armor and weapons they used. Then he used his imagination to conjure up the setting: a

dramatic sky and a fairytale town in the distance.

Composing (arranging) a picture that includes this number of people takes great skill and planning. Altdorfer came up with the idea of using a "bird's-eye view." By painting the scene as if it was seen from a distance and from a great height, he was able to fit in more. He created a panoramic view.

Fields of glory

When kings and rulers go to war, they want glory and to have that glory and honor recorded. Nowadays, photographers take pictures that show exactly what happens but in the past, artists did the job. They were paid to paint the victor's triumph, regardless of the truth. The ruler wasn't interested in showing his subjects and future generations how many people died; he wanted to impress them with the size of his army and the scale of his victory.

Even a small victory might command a great

▶ *This picture represents battle as a glorious event. The artist wanted to show the scale and splendor of the conflict, so he painted a panoramic view in a dramatic setting. The plaque in the sky tells us in Latin that the picture is of Alexander the Great defeating King Darius III of Persia (you can see them in the center of the throng). How can you tell what time of day it is?*
[Alexander the Great's Last Battle, *Albrecht Altdorfer*]

ALEXANDER M DARIVM VIT: SVPERAT
CÆSIS IN ACIE PERSAR: PEDIT: CM.EQVIT
VERO X.M.IN TERFECTIS. MATRE.QVOQVE
CONIVGE.LIBERIS DARII REGVM H.AVD
AMPLIVS EQVITIB: FVGA DILAPSI.CAPTIS.

painting. *The Rout of San Romano,* by the Florentine artist Paolo Uccello (above), was a picture of a minor skirmish in which the Florentine army beat the Sienese. Uccello painted it for the ruler of Florence, Lorenzo de Medici, to go on the wall of his bedchamber. Consequently it showed the Florentine army as fearless men, riding the best horses and wearing the finest armor.

A new perspective

Uccello's painting is best known for its use of perspective, a new technique that fascinated Uccello and other 15th-century artists such as Filippo Brunelleschi and Leon Battista Alberti. Perspective enables an artist to make objects look as though they are three-dimensional, even though they are drawn or painted on a flat surface. At its simplest it means that the farther away something is, the smaller it is drawn or painted in the picture. By using perspective, Uccello created figures that look solid rather than flat. The figures at the front of his battle scene look as though they are nearer to you than the ones at the back. It is almost as though the figures in the distance are running into the wall behind the picture.

▲ *In this battle scene, the artist has not attempted to show the horrors of war. He is more concerned to create a three-dimensional quality, using the new (to him) technique of perspective. Despite the soldier lying on the ground, no screams can be heard from these combatants. They look more like wooden figures from a funfair than living human beings on the field of battle.*
[The Rout of San Romano, *Paolo Uccello*]

▼ *The Battle of Lepanto in 1571 was the last sea battle fought with galleys (boats with oars). Three hundred of them clashed near Greece. Imagine the churning of the blood-soaked sea, the noise of gunfire and explosions, the smoke and the confusion. How well has the artist captured the scene? Does the battle look convincing? How has the artist used perspective? Does the immense amount of detail make the painting more or less realistic?* [The Battle of Lepanto, 7 October 1571]

In memoriam

Look for statues of commanders or generals in the place where you live. Do you recognize them without looking at their names? See if you can find out what they did and why they stand so grandly or sit so proudly on their horses in the middle of the town.

Also, look for memorials to local people who died for their country in wars this century. Many are plain, decorated only with wreaths. Others have sculpted figures on them – often the figure of Liberty or the winged figure of Victory. Look at the figures. Are they realistic or symbolic? Read the names on the memorial. How do they make you feel? How would you design a memorial?

The carnival of war

With its bright colors and robust figures, *The Rout of San Romano* is more like a pageant (a colorful procession) than a war. The same is true of *The Battle of Lepanto* (below), an early painting of a famous sea battle.

There were many naval battles during the 15th and 16th centuries. Huge fleets of ships and many sailors were involved. Paintings of such conflicts showed the number of ships and the scale of the battle. The ruling monarch hung the painting in a public place so the victory could be seen by as many people as possible. Art was one of the few ways of communicating news and making powerful

men appear even more important and powerful.

As time passed, marine paintings were not so stiff and formal. Ships looked less like diagrams and artists paid greater attention to the movement of the waves and clouds, and to the effect of light on a scene. They realized that light changes the appearance of all it touches, giving each object form and depth. This made the fury of battle more believable.

Lest we forget

Pictures bear witness to an event, but because they are hung indoors, they must be visited to be seen. Public monuments, however, can be seen by everybody as they go about their daily business. Since ancient times, columns, arches and statues concerned with war have been erected in towns and cities. Some commemorate great victories: l'Arc de Triomphe in Paris, for instance, is covered with sculptures that tell of Napoleon's conquests.

Modern war memorials rarely glorify victories. Their intention is to honor the dead and wounded. First and Second World War memorials

The Statue of Liberty

Both the American and the French people had to fight for their liberty, the Americans for independence from the British, the French against the tyranny of their unjust aristocracy.

To commemorate the centenary of the Declaration of Independence, the French sculptor Auguste Bartholdi created a giant statue to be given to the people of the United States by the people of France. The huge figure of Liberty was erected on an island in New York Bay and stands as a symbol to immigrants of the freedom they would find in the United States, safe from oppression, poverty and conflict. Stepping out of broken chains, Liberty holds the torch of freedom in her right hand as a welcoming beacon. At 305ft (93m) high including the pedestal, the statue is one of the largest in the world.

History tells us that statues have been built since ancient times. The Colossus of Rhodes was one of the Seven Wonders of the Ancient World and, like Liberty, held a torch. It was a giant figure constructed to commemorate the lifting of a yearlong siege of the island of Rhodes.

Near and far

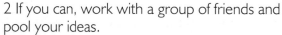

Although Altdorfer's panoramic view of a battle (page 11) is exciting, it is not disturbing and horrifying as the event itself must have been. Only a close-up tells the human story of war and suffering. Draw a war scene in two ways, first visualized from a distance and then from close at hand.

What you need
- large sheets of paper
- sketch pad
- Tape
- pencils, paints, paintbrushes or any painting material you prefer.

What you do
For the panoramic scene:
1 Read an account of an old battle in a book, or a modern one in a newspaper, or watch one on the television news.

2 If you can, work with a group of friends and pool your ideas.
3 Imagine the numbers of soldiers and civilians, tanks, planes and weapons in the conflict. Imagine the destruction of the land or buildings. Sketch individual elements of your picture and work out how you are going to get them all in. Probably you will have to paint them very small.
4 Tape your paper on the wall, draw in the whole scene, then paint it. How does it look?

For the close-up:
1 Now focus on a small part of the big picture – perhaps where there is a wounded soldier, a lost child or an exploding weapon. (Each person in the group can take a different part.)
2 Paint the fragment in detail concentrating on the feelings and suffering of the people.
3 Compare your close-up with the panorama. Which tells you more about the battle? Which tells you more about war?

can be found in towns and cities all over Europe. In Washington D.C. there is a monument to all the Americans who died in the Vietnam War. The names of the victims are inscribed on a long, sweeping wall. The somber simplicity of the monument is moving and beautiful.

The front line

The purpose of pictures that made war look glamorous and exciting was not just to glorify the rulers. It was also to inspire and encourage young men to go willingly to war and fight. Only when they reached the front line did they find out the truth. If they had known what they were in for, and had any choice whether to go or not, many would have stayed at home.

Gradually more realism crept into pictures of war. The figures in the picture of the Battle of Agincourt, below, still look like toys but they do show terrible injuries and how brutal hand-to-hand combat was. Later, artists put even more realism into their pictures and expressed their own feelings about war.

A passionate heart

The 19th-century French painter Henri Rousseau felt passionately that war was a terrible evil. During his lifetime he had seen much suffering. His grandfather

◀ *This illustration comes from a 15th-century chronicle (record of events). The knights look like puppets or toy soldiers and there is no blood, but nonetheless the artist has been at pains to show the twisted mutilation of the wounded. The violence of the battle contrasts with the peaceful landscape in the background.* [Battle of Agincourt from St Alban's Chronicle]

▲ This is a picture of utter destruction. War is symbolized as a horsewoman riding over a heap of corpses whose flesh is being pecked at by ravens. The black figure of the horse with its strange long head looks sinister against the colorful sky. The figure at the front with the moustache is said to be a self-portrait of the artist, Henri Rousseau. Why do you think he has included himself in the picture?
[War. It Passes, Terrifying, Leaving Despair, Tears and Ruins Everywhere, *Henri Rousseau*]

had been killed fighting in Algeria. France had suffered a swift and bloody defeat by the Prussians in the Franco-Prussian War (1870-1871). Rousseau himself had witnessed assassinations and bombings by anarchists in Paris in 1890.

"When a king wants to go to war," said Rousseau, "a mother must go to him and order him not to do it." Rousseau believed that a painter, even more than a mother, might have the power to change people's minds. He tried to do this by painting antiwar pictures such as the one above.

Rousseau had no formal art training. He taught himself to paint. For most of his life he worked in the customs office in Paris and did not paint full-time until he retired. Artists who have had no professional training are called naïve artists, or Primitives. Because of his lack of training, Rousseau feared that some critics would not take his work seriously. A way to prevent this, he thought, was to paint a subject as serious as the horror of war.

Rousseau was not concerned to paint a realistic picture. He did not go to war to see for himself what it was like. Instead he used his imagination to get across the meaning of war and depict violence in a way that was striking and unusual. His war picture is a symbolic account of a battle, the figure on the horse is a symbol of war.

In the firing line

Unlike Rousseau, the British artists of World War I (1914-1918) saw the war for themselves. Like thousands of other men, they willingly joined the fighting. At the beginning of the war, nobody knew how bad it was going to be. Some even saw it as a welcome opportunity. The artist Wyndham Lewis wrote: "You must not miss a war, if one is going! You cannot afford to miss the experience."

The Futurists

The artist Christopher Nevinson began the war full of enthusiastic zeal. He was the only English member of a group of artists called the Futurists, who had come together in Italy. The Futurists believed that war was a glorious thing. Nevinson's early pictures (see below) take a positive view. They show the power of war with human beings as efficient parts in the war machine. Nevinson emphasized this with bright colors and bold shapes.

For much of the war Nevinson worked with the Red Cross. He experienced many things that changed his view of war. In the course of his work, he saw men injured and disfigured, others driven

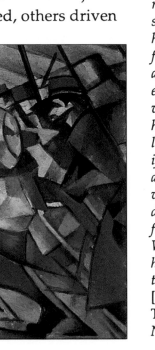

▼ *These soldiers are wearing the red caps and trousers of the French Infantry. The artist Christopher Nevinson has painted the figures as one block, moving as if they are a single person. Although he has shown many figures, few have faces and these have little expression. The artist wanted to show how human beings had to lose their individuality if they were to become an effective part of the war machine. Notice the diagonal lines of the figures and the muskets. What effect do they have? What feelings do they arouse?* [Returning to the Trenches, *Christopher Nevinson*]

Shortly before the outbreak of World War II, the Nazi party in Germany produced a powerful piece of propaganda. Adolf Hitler, leader of the party, asked the film maker Leni Reifensthal to film the 1934 party congress in Nuremberg. Her film *Triumph of the Will* is a masterful piece of artistic direction that makes the Nazi party look invincible and glorious. It begins with Hitler descending from the skies, his plane shadowed against the clouds, and continues with rousing scenes of rallies and speeches. It was such a powerful piece of propaganda that after the war it was banned. The democratic government of Germany felt that it might still have the power to inspire those who watched it to form a new Nazi party.

mad by shellshock. His attitude to the conflict and to his art changed. His paintings became softer and grimmer. They showed the wounded and dying as real people in real pain.

The landscape of war

Two artist brothers, John and Paul Nash, joined up full of a sense of "doing the right thing" for their country. They enlisted in the Artists' Rifles (a regiment which was only for artists) and fought in the trenches in France. John painted the appalling scenes

▲ *This picture is surprisingly calm considering that it is the evening after a day's fighting. There are no dead bodies in the painting, no wounded men, no sense of chaos or human misery. And yet there is desolation and destruction. Can you explain how the artist John Nash has conveyed this feeling? What do you think he considered the most devastating impact of the war?*
[Oppy Wood, *John Nash*]

he witnessed from memory. Paul sketched what he saw at the front and turned the sketches into paintings when he returned home. He showed the devastation and desolation of the landscape wrought by the war.

The right image

Christopher Nevinson and the Nash brothers were official British War Artists. They were commissioned and paid by the Ministry of Information to record the war. They were not expected to lie about what they saw or to glorify it, but some of their paintings were used for propaganda. Propaganda is the use of words and images to influence how people think. Governments use propaganda to gain popularity for themselves and show their enemies and opponents in a bad light.

At the start of World War I, the British government produced posters and leaflets that presented a positive view of the war. Artists painted

I WANT YOU FOR U.S. ARMY

NEAREST RECRUITING STATION

▲ This World War I recruiting poster shows how art can be used by the state. Uncle Sam (a nickname for the United States, taken from its initials) looks straight into the eyes of any young American who happens to pass. If you had been thinking about joining up, how would the poster have made you feel?
[I Want You for U.S. Army, *James Montgomery Flagg*]

Family fortunes

There are many people alive today who can remember World War II and more recent wars in Korea, Vietnam, the Middle East and elsewhere. Ask older members of your family to tell you their experiences. They may have fought themselves or helped with casualties, worked in munitions factories or on the land, or simply waited anxiously for their loved ones to return. See if they have any souvenirs of the war, such as leaflets, photographs, ration books, gas masks, old documents or newspapers.

Write down what you discover in a scrapbook. Illustrate your account with your own drawings and with photocopies of photographs and documents. You may even be inspired to write a poem inspired by your collection.

The poetry of war

While artists recorded the events of World War I in pictures, poets who went to war painted pictures in words. Their poems describe the war vividly and poignantly, with images of the battle-scarred landscape and the wretchedness of the trenches. Read this poem by Siegfried Sassoon and see what pictures form in your mind. Then draw or paint a picture of what you "see." Your picture can depict the whole poem or you may feel inspired by just one line. Try the first two lines: "At dawn the ridge emerges massed and dun/In the wild purple of the glow'ring sun." or "Lines of grey, muttering faces, masked with fear." Think whether you want to make your painting an abstract impression of a scene or realistic, with plenty of detail.

Attack!

At dawn the ridge emerges massed and dun
In the wild purple of the glow'ring sun,
Smouldering through spouts of drifting smoke that shroud
The menacing scarred slope; and, one by one,
Tanks creep and topple forward to the wire.
The barrage roars and lifts. Then clumsily bowed
With bombs and guns and shovels and battle-gear,
Men jostle and climb to meet the bristling fire.
Lines of grey, muttering faces, masked with fear,
They leave their trenches, going over the top,
While time ticks blank and busy on their wrists,
And hope, with furtive eyes and grappling fists,
Flounders in mud. O Jesus make it stop.

[Siegfried Sassoon, 1886-1967]

images of brave, victorious soldiers and their defeated enemies. It was important that men continued to join the army and that people felt that they were on the winning side. The government believed that if they knew the truth, they would be demoralized.

In the United States, there was a strong antiwar feeling. People did not want to become involved in a foreign war. When the government finally decided to enter the war in 1917, it had to create enthusiasm for the war effort.

American propaganda showed the war as a battle for freedom and democracy against a fearsome, tyrannical enemy. Artists painted handsome US soldiers fighting for their family and friends at home. But in other pictures the faces were evil. They were of the "Huns" (Germans) hell-bent on destroying civilization. A famous US army recruitment poster (opposite) pointed the finger at all who avoided their responsibility. It appealed to people's patriotism and made them ashamed not to enlist.

4 Counting the cost

War has a far-reaching effect. The damage it causes is not restricted to those who fight. Ordinary people are affected too. Towns and cities are destroyed. Civilians are killed or are made homeless and hungry or fall victim to disease.

For a long time, nobody chose the consequences of war as the subject for art. Artists had to please the people who paid for their paintings. No one wanted to pay for pictures that showed bloodshed, suffering and death.

▼ *Goya hoped that this painting would keep alive the memory of the Spanish patriots who were shot defending their country against Napoleon. He deliberately exaggerated the horror of the scene by using harsh light and violent brushstrokes. The soldiers are faceless and ruthless, while the expressions of the terrified, defenseless townspeople show their disbelieving horror and outrage. Some cover their faces. The central figure raises his hands like Christ on the cross, his eyes wide with terror. The effect is violent and brutal.*
[Third of May, 1808 (the Executions), *Francisco Goya*]

The disasters of war

In the days when most artists compliantly painted what their patrons wanted, one artist stood out from the rest. Francisco Goya was employed by the Spanish royal family (whose portraits he painted), but he had enough freedom to choose subjects of his own. He felt strongly about the evils of war, which he had seen when Napoleon's troops invaded Spain at the beginning of the 19th century.

His series of etchings called *The Disasters of War* shows scenes of French troops suppressing the Spanish resistance to Napoleon. The atrocities he illustrated are brutal and chilling. Goya wanted to alert people to the cruelty that existed in the minds of men. One of his greatest paintings, *Third of May, 1808 (the Executions)*, opposite, shocked many people when it went on public display. Nothing like it had been seen before. It shows Napoleon's soldiers shooting, at close range, Spanish civilians who had fought against them to defend their city.

Innocent casualties

A century later, another Spanish artist, Pablo Picasso, felt equally moved by a barbaric episode in his country's history. In 1936, the left-wing Spanish government was attacked by the right-wing General Franco. The country was thrown into a bloody civil war that lasted three years. Franco used aggressive tactics including bombing small towns into oblivion. One of these towns was called Guernica.

Picasso was outraged by the senseless killing of ordinary people and the destruction of their homes. He was asked to paint a mural for the Spanish pavilion of an international exhibition, and he chose the bombing of Guernica as its subject.

By using a series of powerful images (a mother with her dead child, a dead fighter with a broken sword, a horse frenzied with fear), Picasso evoked the horror of war and its consequences, in a manner that was startingly unusual and vivid.

The camera at war

One reason why *Guernica* has such a strong impact is because it combines different moments from the bombing and shows them to us all at once.

Photography, on the other hand, can only show us one event at a time. Nevertheless, it is an effective means of recording events and has the advantage of speed. A photographer can go right into the action, take a picture, and get away quickly. A dramatic moment can be captured in an instant.

The first war to be photographed extensively was the American Civil War (1861-65). Matthew Brady and his ten assistants took 7,000 photographs of it, travelling

▼ The young soldier in this photograph was killed over 100 years ago during the American Civil War. Like a painting, a photograph often has to be carefully composed. The photographer made sure the figure was in the center of his lens and stood well back from him so that the rocks created a dramatic setting. The effect is shocking: the lonely figure of the soldier is a powerful symbol of the waste created by war. [Dead Sharp Shooter, Matthew Brady]

to all the battlefronts. Brady had trained as an artist and saw things through an artist's eye. He knew what would make a good picture.

Brady and other photographers took pictures of all aspects of the war: weapons and fortifications, officers and troops, the wounded and the dead. Unlike Goya and Picasso, they were driven not by a sense of outrage but by a desire to record the war faithfully. Their honest, unflinching photographs are as moving as many paintings.

Art from hell on earth
Even in the dreadful conditions of the Nazi concentration camps (page 26), people drew and painted pictures. In a museum in Prague there is an exhibition of art by the children of the Treblinka camp. Some of the pictures were drawn on tiny scraps of material or card with broken pencils or even dirt. See if you can find examples of art by people who have been imprisoned. What does their work tell you about their lives and thoughts?

The ultimate horror

Photographic images of war have an immediate impact on those who see them. Often they have the power to change the course of history. Who knows what would have happened if the world had seen photographs taken inside the Nazi concentration camps of World War II.

When the war was over, British and American troops liberated the camps. They were joined by photographers, and by artists such as Eric Taylor who documented the horror of what they saw. Their pictures of emaciated prisoners, dying of starvation and disease, remind us of the cruelty that humans are capable of.

◄ *This woman's face and emaciated body say more about what she has experienced than any words could express. She has just been released from the Nazi concentration camp at Belsen. This is a rough sketch only, not a finished painting. Do you think a painting would have been any more moving?* [Liberated from Belsen, *Eric Taylor*]

Conflict in collage

Picasso's *Guernica* is a collage. It was made by pasting pieces of paper of different colors and patterns on to a plain background.

Choose a subject and make a collage yourself. It can be of violent events from the newspapers or television, or a fight or quarrel that you have witnessed. Make a picture or a mural on your own or with friends.

What you need
- different types of paper with a variety of textures, e.g., corrugated cardboard, glossy wrapping paper, newspaper
- glue, scissors
- paint and paintbrushes
- large piece of stiff card

What you do
1 Plan your picture by drawing outlines of figures and shapes with a pencil on the large card.
2 Cut out shapes from the different pieces of paper to fit your composition. Make some of the edges jagged and some smooth, to vary the texture.
3 Paint facial features and other details with a brush. Try glueing on string, pieces of fabric, aluminum foil and other materials to add even more interest and texture.

Protest and revolution

◀ *The figure in the middle of this picture, carrying the French flag and a bayoneted rifle, represents Liberty. She is leading a young urchin, a member of the middle classes (in top hat) and a working-class man from the smoking ruins to victory and freedom. This is a large picture: the corpses at the front of it are life size. Imagine what it is like to stand in front of it.* [Liberty Leading the People, *Eugène Delacroix*]

Where there is great injustice, conflict can be a power for good. For instance, if a tyrannical government or a ruler will not respond to reasonable argument, removing it by force may be the only course of action.

Revolution and romance

In the early 19th century, the people of France were ruled by Louis XVIII and then Charles X, both of whom were unpopular. In 1830, in order to get rid of Charles X, they rose up in revolution. After a bloody struggle he was deposed. The artist Eugène Delacroix was inspired by this example of people overcoming their rulers and used it as inspiration for his picture *Liberty Leading the People* (above).

This painting, with its heroic figure of Liberty leading a scruffy band of revolutionaries to freedom, was itself revolutionary. Unlike other artists of the time, Delacroix wasn't interested in perfection. He painted with dashing brushstrokes to create

Drawing on stone

When Daumier drew his cartoons for the newspaper, he began by drawing them on a slab of stone. This is the first step in a method of printing called lithography. Daumier drew his pictures on the stone with a piece of greasy chalk. Then he soaked the stone with water. Because water and grease don't mix, the water ran off the drawing leaving it dry but the stone wet. Daumier then inked the stone with a greasy ink that clung to his drawn lines. He laid a piece of paper on the stone and pressed it down hard. The finished lithograph was an exact replica of what Daumier had first drawn on the stone.

Lithography is still used in printing today but of course it has become more sophisticated. The slab of stone has been replaced by a zinc plate and images are transferred to the plate photographically.

movement and life.

This attitude to art was was known as Romanticism. Romantic artists were more concerned with showing feelings than attaining perfection. Like Goya before him, Delacroix didn't hesitate to paint the dirty feet of the dead or the dishevelled clothing of the revolutionaries. These details from ordinary life help us to understand what the figures are experiencing emotionally.

▼ *Read the title of this picture first. The scene takes place in a prison. The artist wanted to show the cruel conditions that existed there. The wardens are shown as grotesque and*

Cartoon crusader

The Romantics also felt that it was important for artists to express their beliefs. Honoré Daumier, a French artist, did this by drawing political cartoons for the newspapers. One caricature of the king so offended His Majesty that Daumier was imprisoned for drawing it.

In his cartoons, Daumier exposed the injustices he saw around him. He was appalled by the greed and corruption

overfed, especially when compared to the dying prisoner. Why is it "safe" to release this prisoner?
[It's Safe to Release This One, *Honoré Daumier*]

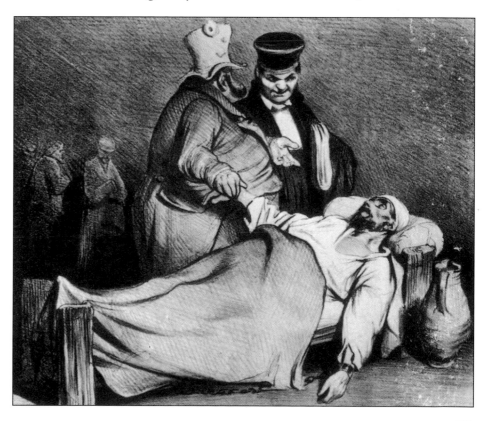

of those in high office. Unlike Delacroix, he drew with precise lines and careful shading. He made lithographs (see page 29) of everyday scenes, such as travellers in a railway carriage. He preferred ordinary subjects to the grander subjects chosen by Delacroix.

Public art in Mexico

Newspaper cartoons like Daumier's are an effective way of getting an idea across to a large number of people. Other artists have also used cartoons to inspire revolution and protest. Mexico's Revolution of 1910-1929 was a popular uprising against a dictatorship that had taken land from the people and removed their right to vote. Diego Rivera and José

▲ *The man with a moustache and a band of bullets around his chest is Emiliano Zapata, one of the leaders of the Mexican Revolution. His followers are marching along in front of him. Notice how the artist has repeated the same lines of the legs of the marchers to suggest movement. Compare this picture with the one by Christopher Nevinson on page 18. Can you see any similarities in the style of the figures and the lines of the paintings?*
[Zapatistas Marching Led by Emiliano Zapata and Pancho Villa During the Mexican Revolution, *José Orozco*]

Clemente Orozco, two Mexican artists of the period, drew political cartoons for magazines that supported the revolution. They also painted large, colorful murals of revolutionary subjects for all the people to see.

Rivera and Orozco believed that art belonged on the outside walls of public buildings, not tucked away in galleries where only a few people saw it. They were inspired by the Communist artists in the Soviet Union whose strong posters and wall paintings communicated directly to ordinary people. The Mexican murals showed scenes from the country's troubled history and the heroes of the Revolution – Emiliano Zapata and Pancho Villa. These murals, with their bright colors and strong images, still survive as a record of Mexico's history.

Real life in the USA

Over the border, in the United States, artists such as Ben Shahn were impressed by the work of these Mexicans. They liked their bold way of painting and the fact that Rivera and Orozco wanted to change things with their paintings, particularly the way people thought.

America at this time (the 1930s) was in the middle of the Great Depression. Many people were starving and homeless. Unemployment was high and food was in short supply. One group of artists painted pictures that showed this poverty. Because these paintings were so realistic and concerned with the daily life of ordinary people, the artists were called Social Realists.

Social Realists wanted to alert the public to the hardships suffered during the Depression. This, they hoped, would lead to new government policies that would improve living conditions.

Art and politics

Take a look at political cartoons and caricatures in current newspapers and magazines. Are they as hard-hitting as Daumier's were? Are they as well drawn? Do they make you laugh? Do they make you think? Try drawing caricatures yourself. Draw one of someone you dislike and someone you like. Which is easier?

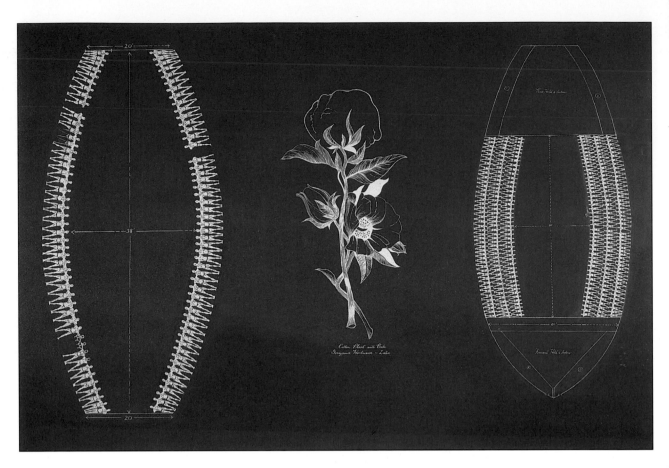

Cotton Plant with Pods
Gossypium Herbaceum – Latin

During the 1960s – another time of protest – the American civil rights movement, which aimed to stamp out racism, was born. Artists were important members of the movement, and even formed groups of their own.

Malcolm Bailey was an artist who believed passionately in civil rights. His *Untitled* (above) points to social injustices of the past. It makes people think about the inequalities between white people and black people that still exist. Like all other artists of protest and revolution,

Bailey hoped his work would help create a future without injustice.

The struggle continues

Artists today continue to use their talent to highlight causes or injustices. Sometimes they lend their name to a charity and create artwork for that charity to sell. Alternatively, they might feel strongly enough about an issue to design a poster or make a video. Many artists have helped with the work of the charity Amnesty International, for example.

▲ *This picture looks like a simple pattern. It is, in fact, based on a diagram that showed how the maximum number of human beings could be crammed into a ship. African slaves, cruelly chained and ill-fed, were transported on such ships to pick cotton in America (a cotton plant is shown in the center). The slaves had no rights and no individual identity. By showing this so simply, the artist makes us appreciate the cruelty and inhumanity of the slave trade. [Untitled 1969, Malcolm Bailey]*

32

Plaster heroes

Decide on a hero or heroine you could immortalize in plaster. We have used Emiliano Zapata.

What you need
- plaster of Paris
- cardboard box (e.g., a shoe box) with no holes
- table knife
- small piece of wire
- poster or powder paint, paintbrushes

What you do

1 Mix the plaster of Paris thoroughly and pour it into the cardboard box.

2 As the plaster sets, design your figure on a piece of paper. Make it fill as much of the plaster shape as possible and keep it simple.

3 When the plaster has set, turn it out of the box. You now have a block to carve.

4 Transfer your design on to the plaster block by drawing round it with a pencil.

5 Use the knife to shape the block. Carve around the outline of the figure. Leave the bottom of the block uncarved so that your figure stands firmly. Carve details such as facial features and textures on the clothes using the wire.

6 Paint your figure and watch it come to life. (You'll need to make the paint extra thick and bright because plaster absorbs paint very easily.)

6 Inward battles

Conflict is not confined to the battlefield. It exists all around us – in our friendships, in our families, at school, at work, in our hearts and in our minds.

Sometimes we fight with those we love best. Look at the picture of a husband and wife fighting (right). This was drawn 600 years ago but it still looks modern. Put the couple in contemporary clothes and give the woman a rolling pin instead of a distaff (a rod used to spin wool), and this could be a modern picture, a sexist cartoon in a newspaper, for instance.

This picture was drawn in the margin of a book of psalms, called a psalter. All the words and the pictures in the psalter were drawn by monks. The pictures in the margins (called marginalia) show scenes from everyday life all those years ago. The main picture illustrated a scene from the Bible.

Marginalia, like the example here, were often lighthearted and humorous, although many had a serious point to make.

▲ The artist of this scene has shown the emotions of the husband and wife in their stances and in their facial expressions – their downturned mouths. He has exaggerated the proportions of the wife to make her look especially fierce – see how long her legs are. In contrast, the husband is crouching and apologetic. It is easy to see who is the stronger character here. With simple lines and exaggerated movement, the artist has captured the scene exactly – rather like a modern cartoon. [Wife beating her husband with a distaff, Luttrell Psalter]

The inner person

Medieval artists were hindered in their attempts to tackle the dilemmas and conflicts of existence by having to use techniques and materials that were not very sophisticated. Pictures of that time tended to look flat and the figures two-dimensional. Moreover, artists had not yet learned how to illustrate deep feelings and emotions, except in a simple, uncomplicated way.

▼ *Jesus, praying before his crucifixion, is about to be betrayed by Judas who is approaching with soldiers from the back of the picture. In painting the rounded, realistic figures, especially those of the disciples, Mantegna was influenced by Greek sculpture. The landscape reinforces the emotional impact of the painting. The sky is heavy with foreboding, the rocks in the landscape twist and turn as though in anguish. A solitary bird watches like a dark omen.*
[Agony in the Garden, Andrea Mantegna]

This all changed during a period called the Renaissance – an influential style of painting that started in Italy and spread through northern Europe in the 14th and 15th centuries. Renaissance means "rebirth" and in this case it referred to the rebirth of classical (ancient Greek and Roman) ideas in art and teaching. Painters and sculptors based the poses and clothes of their figures on classical statues. For the first time, they began to portray the feelings of the people in their paintings and figures began to look more human.

Images of conflict

When two people confront each other during an argument, they stand in an aggressive way and wear hostile expressions.

Posters advertising films often show people fighting or arguing. See if you can find any. Look especially for posters of Indian love films, where the actors and actresses are often portrayed in the grip of a deep emotion. Also look in books with stills (photographs) taken from old black and white movies. Use the expressions and postures you see as a starting point for a painting.

Depth of feeling

Andrea Mantegna was a Renaissance artist who knew how to show conflict in the human mind. His picture of the *Agony in the Garden* (page 35) shows Jesus in the Garden of Gethsemene on the morning of his crucifixion. Jesus is praying alone as his disciples sleep. The Bible describes him as "sorrowful and very heavy." He is facing an inner conflict. He knows he is to have a painful death which is necessary to save the souls of mankind, but he would rather avoid it. Mantegna uses color and landscape to reflect Jesus' state of mind.

A tortured soul

Four hundred years later, a Norwegian artist, Edvard Munch, also used landscape to reflect mood. He twisted it about and painted it in evocative colors that echoed the feelings of his figures. All his pictures are about emotional states, usually melancholy or depressive ones. Munch was particularly good at illustrating the inner battles of the human mind.

The Frieze of Life was a series of paintings in which

▲ *The man at the front of this picture is suffering from jealousy. The woman he loves is walking along the beach in the distance with another man. How does the artist get the feeling of jealousy across? Do you think the colors he has chosen match the mood of the man? [Melancholy (the Yellow Boat), Edvard Munch]*

Munch showed the different stages of a love affair. He begins by showing attraction, then union but, as the love affair goes wrong, quickly proceeds to jealousy and despair. His paintings of jealousy, such as *Melancholy (the Yellow Boat)* (above), capture the conflict and misery of a mind torn between love and hate.

The Expressionists

We have seen how Edvard Munch used color and landscape to pack his pictures with highly charged emotion. This method of painting was taken even further by a group of German painters called the Expressionists. They wanted to express their feelings directly on to canvas. They did this by using violent, surprising colors and distorted shapes. Famous Expressionists include Oskar Kokoschka and Franz Marc. Eventually artists went even further and expressed their feelings without painting objects at all – just colors and shapes. This was called abstract art.

▲ *The women in this picture have gathered to watch the men go to war. You can see them marching past on the left. The artist has shown what war means to those left at home. Can you imagine from their expressions what the women are thinking? With its richly painted fabrics and polished surfaces, this painting is very different from Munch's. Here the background is just a setting for the figures. Which of the two pictures do you think better conveys the feelings of the people in it?*
[War, *Anna Lea Merritt*]

Sentimental stories

At the same time in Victorian England, many artists also dwelt on the agonies of life. A group of artists called the Pre-Raphaelites, for example, often included a moral as a subject for their painting.

Anna Lea Merritt, in her picture *War* (above), shows a fearful wife who has just seen her husband leave to fight for his country. This picture is more realistic than Munch's but is just as effective at showing the confused emotions.

Your feelings in paint

Think of deep emotions that you feel from time to time. Choose from anger, jealousy, frustration, sadness, depression, joy. Try expressing those feelings in abstract paintings. To get started you could look at a picture that moves you, or read the poem by Siegfried Sassoon in Chapter 3 again – or read other poetry. You might like to do this activity with a group of friends. Discuss your feelings about a particular painting or poem. Do you all feel the same way about it?

What you need

- paper
- paintbrushes of different thicknesses
- water
- paints (watercolors and poster), pastels, crayons, charcoal

What you do

Think of ways of expressing different emotions, using bright or somber colors, different techniques and materials. Think hard how best to match your emotion. For example, for a happy picture, you might choose poster paints in primary colors, whereas sadness may inspire you to do a gentle watercolor in pastels. Anger? Perhaps a heavy, charcoal drawing with wild strokes. Depression? An etching scratched on a thick layer of black wax crayon.

Only a game

Sports and games are enjoyable forms of conflict. Nevertheless they can cause bitter feelings between contestants, who may even resort to physical violence because their emotions and desire to win run so high. How often do you hear someone say, "It's only a game!", while trying to reduce the violent feelings that have been aroused?

Good sports

The ancient Greeks and Romans enjoyed all manner of sports and competition. Their greatest heroes were warriors, and their gods were constantly at odds with each other. The Greeks invented the Olympic games; they were also the first people to elect their leaders. Their philosophers loved to dispute with each other. All these kinds of competition are celebrated in their art. Athletes often feature on their vases, and artists enjoyed representing the human form in combat. Their epic poems are full of tales of champion runners.

▼ *There is a lot of energy in this picture although the figures are quite static. Look at the way the arm of the boxer on the left is pulled back ready to strike. These young boxers decorated the walls of an ancient palace in Knossos, Crete. They belonged to a race of people called the Minoans, whose civilization was at its peak from 2200 BC to 1450 BC. The palace had many other wall paintings (called frescoes) showing different scenes from Minoan life.* [Knossos Palace: Fresco of the Boxing Children, *1500 BC*]

▶ *This unappealing crowd of men is playing billiards for money. They are dressed in fancy tailored jackets with big cuffs and gold buttons, like the dress uniforms of officers. But these men are not brave enough to fight in real wars. They are men of leisure who idly squander time and money. The artist has deliberately drawn the characters as ugly caricatures to make gambling seem unattractive. The picture is an etching. Look at the hundreds of lines the artist has drawn. He has shown shadows by drawing parallel lines in one direction, then crossing them with parallel lines in the other. This is called cross-hatching. [Billiards, R. Sayer]*

Dressed to kill

When the outcome of a game gives the winner only glory, competition is fierce enough.

When money is involved, the contestants' feelings can be murderous. The men in the etching (above) of a billiard

Etching

Billiards by R. Sayer (above) is an etching. Etching is a technique that enables an artist to produce a large number of images quickly and cheaply. To make an etching, a metal plate is coated with a layer of resin. The artist then draws his picture into the resin with a needle. The plate is dipped into acid which bites away the exposed lines. The plate is inked, the ink settling into the new lines, and a print is taken by pressing paper on to the plate.

One of the advantages of etching is that it is possible to draw very fine detail – much more so than with a paintbrush. In the 18th century, etchings were sold cheaply in shops and by printmakers. They were displayed in homes throughout the country and were almost as popular as posters are today. Artists still use the technique of etching. It enables them to produce several copies of the same image.

game, for example, can't be described as "true" sportsmen. There is no fun-loving friendship on their faces. They are drawn as grotesque caricatures who care only for money.

Prints like this were popular in 18th-century England. Artists, such as Thomas Rowlandson and William Hogarth, made etchings that told a story with a moral that would teach a lesson to those tempted by immorality. Subjects of these prints included the evils of playing sport for money, like the one shown on page 41, and the attraction of evil. Often there were several prints (a series) telling a story.

Hidden tension

Anyone who has played the game of croquet knows that it can be quite vicious, with one player targeting another and malleting their ball into the flowerbeds. But the women in the painting by the American artist Winslow Homer (below) are too polite to play like that. Whatever tensions exist between the players are carefully hidden.

Homer had painted the American Civil War earlier in his career, so he was accustomed to recording scenes of conflict. He also painted wild and turbulent seascapes full of movement

▼ *There is not much activity in this picture. The only movement comes from the wind. The artist has captured the freshness and light of life outdoors, but the women seem at odds with the scene: they would be happier taking tea than playing ball games. Compare their leisurely languor with the energy and tension of the figures drawn by Sérusier and Beckmann (see pages 43 and 44).* [Croquet Scene, *Winslow Homer*]

and vigor. But here, at home, in this tranquil scene, he chose to portray American life as one filled with wealth, health and happiness.

Rough and tumble

Max Beckmann's *Football Players* (left) couldn't be more different from the croquet party. You can feel the violence of their struggle almost as if you were among them. During World War I Beckmann, a German artist, had served in the medical corps. He was so distressed by his harrowing experiences that he suffered a nervous breakdown. In some of his paintings, his figures seem to reflect his state of mind, so tense are their muscles and so determined the expressions on their faces. Perhaps at the sportsfield, he could not help recalling the battlefield.

◀ *Max Beckmann liked to paint long, thin pictures. He also liked to place his figures on top of one another in a topsy-turvy fashion. This works particularly well here as the players struggle for control of the ball. Look at the forlorn figure holding on to the post. Can you see how Beckmann's experiences of the horrors of war might have affected the way he painted this figure in combat?* [Football Players, *Max Beckmann*]

43

Unbeautiful bodies

Ancient Greek and Roman artists, and those of the Renaissance, painted or sculpted their heroes with perfect bodies like those of gods. It was a long time before artists had the freedom to paint bodies as they really are, full of imperfections.

The French artist Paul Sérusier, painting at the turn of this century, showed people of all shapes and sizes, and placed them against striking backgrounds of flat color. He liked to surprise his audience with startling compositions (eg, putting the focal point at the bottom of the picture, not in the center) and distorted figures placed in unexpected positions within the frame. His Breton wrestlers are so involved in their conflict that they become one figure.

The Nabis

Paul Sérusier was a member of a group of artists called the Nabis. (Nabi is a Hebrew word meaning "prophet.") The Nabis wanted to find a simple yet effective style of painting. For inspiration they turned to an earlier French artist, Paul Gauguin, and to Japanese prints. Both of these used large areas of flat color (one color with little shading). The Nabis also liked unusual compositions: the focal point (center of attention) of the picture might be in an unexpected place, at the bottom of the picture perhaps.

Other Nabi artists include Pierre Bonnard and Maurice Denis. Try to find some examples of their work and compare them with the painting by Sérusier. Can you spot the similarities?

▼ *The wrestling figures in this painting are almost caricatures. Their expressions and postures are exaggerated, their feet huge. The picture is divided into two halves: a dark top half and bright yellow bottom half. It is unusual to see a picture with such a large amount of one color. Where do you think the focal point (center of attention) of the painting is? [Wrestling Bretons, Paul Sérusier]*

Computer conflict

How many monsters, aliens and androids have you killed today? How many human beings? When you play a computer game, do you notice the graphics on the screen? Do you notice the colors and contrasts that the games' artists use? Look at some of your games – if you have them – and see how the heroes look compared to the villains. Look at their weapons. When you zap a villain, what happens? Is there blood on the screen or does the victim disappear in a puff of smoke? Does it make violence seem fun? Design the characters for a fantasy game yourself.

Sporting sketches

Practise sketching sports people. They are difficult to draw because they are always moving – even a photographer needs a camera with a very fast shutter speed or the picture will be blurred. Try to capture the feeling of competition. Focus on players in conflict with one another – two people struggling for a ball, perhaps, or facing each other across a net, or running against each other in a race.

What you need
• sports match and players
• sketch book
• pencil or charcoal

What you do
1 Make lightning sketches of figures playing in the match or running a race. It is more important to capture a sense of the action and energy present on the sports field than to produce a finished drawing.
2 Take the sketchbook home and use your drawings as a starting point for a painting. You could develop just one of your sketches or use several. Whichever you choose, remember to try to reproduce the speed, action and conflict of the sports event. And try to show the competitive spirit of the sport.

About the artists

(Only some of the artists are listed below. Some of the works of art in this book are by artists whose names we no longer know.)

ALTDORFER, Albrecht (c. 1480-1538) As well as painting huge pictures, this German artist was also an architect. He was one of the first European artists to paint pictures about nature rather than people.

BAILEY, Malcolm (born 1947) This contemporary black American artist uses art to protest about injustice, particularly racial injustice. He often bases his pictures on diagrams, as he considers this the clearest way to get a message across.

BECKMANN, Max (1884-1950) One of the great figure painters of the 20th century, this German artist belonged to no particular school. His pictures, with their unusual constructions, are unique.

BRADY, Matthew (1823-1896) Originally a painter and portrait photographer, in 1862 Brady organized a group of ten photographers to record the American Civil War.

DAUMIER, Honoré (1808-1879) Although he did paint in oil, Daumier is best known for his newspaper cartoons which poked fun at people in positions of power.

DELACROIX, Eugène (1798-1863) One of the leaders of the French Romantic movement, Delacroix painted with large brushstrokes and vivid color. He filled his pictures with as much feeling and movement as he could.

GOYA y Lucientes, Francisco José de (1746-1828) Goya painted the horrors of Napoleon's occupation of Spain as well as portraits of the Spanish royal family.

HOMER, Winslow (1836-1910) Homer was one of the first American painters to gain international fame. He began as an illustrator, moved on to paint scenes from the daily life of Americans, and ended life as a recluse in Maine, USA, painting seascapes.

MANTEGNA, Andrea (c.1431-1506) This Italian painter and engraver was one of the first artists to use perspective. A court painter, his frescoes were influenced by classical sculpture from ancient Greece.

MERRITT, Anna Lea (1844-1930) Although she was born in Philadelphia, in the USA, Anna Lea Merritt studied in London and travelled widely in Europe. She mostly painted portraits and figure groups.

MUNCH, Edvard (1863-1944) A painter of the darkest human emotions, this Norwegian artist influenced many others, especially the German Expressionists.

NASH, John (1893-1946) A painter of landscapes and plants, he joined his brother Paul Nash in the trenches of World War I as an Official War Artist.

NEVINSON, Christopher (1889-1946) This English artist was influenced by the Italian Futurist painters and, like them, he enjoyed painting machinery and other symbols of the modern age in a strong, angular style.

OROZCO, José Clemente (1883-1949) Originally an architect, this Mexican turned to painting in 1909. His murals show scenes from the lives and history of Mexican people.

PICASSO, Pablo (1881-1973) Picasso was one of the most influential artists of the 20th century. He is well known for his invention, with Georges Braque, of Cubism. He worked in a variety of media, including ceramic, paint and collage.

ROUSSEAU, Henri (1844-1910) This French painter was known as "The Douanier," meaning "customs officer," because that was his occupation. He taught himself to paint by copying paintings in the Louvre museum in Paris. He was immensely proud of his work and thought of himself and Picasso as the "two great painters of the age."

SAYER, Reuben (1815-1888) An etcher of everyday scenes, Sayer was very popular and sold many prints during his lifetime.

SERUSIER, Paul (1884-1927) One of the members of the Nabi group of painters, Sérusier was greatly influenced by Paul Gauguin and by Japanese prints.

TAYLOR, Eric (born 1909) A painter, sculptor, printmaker and teacher, this artist has exhibited all over the world, including Washington D.C. and London.

UCCELLO, Paolo (c.1396-1475) An Italian painter who was fascinated with the problems of how to show three-dimensional (solid) shapes on two-dimensional (flat) surfaces.

Acknowledgments

Zefa, 14; National Gallery of Canada, Gift of the Massey Collection of English Painting, 1946, 18; Library of Congress, 25; Imperial War Museum, London, 26; Collection of Whitney Museum of American Art © 1996, 32; © Nasjonalgalleriet, Oslo, 37.

All other pictures are from the Bridgeman Art Library, courtesy of the following: British Museum, London, 4; British Library, London, 5 (both); Christie's, London, 6; Alte Pinakothek, Munich, 11; National Gallery, London, 12; National Maritime Museum, London, 13; Lambeth Palace Library, London, 16; Musée d'Orsay, Paris/Lauros-Giraudon, 17; Imperial War Museum, London, 19; Imperial War Museum, London, 20; Prado, Madrid, 22; Museo Reina Sofia, Madrid/ Giraudon/© DACS 1996, 23; Louvre, Paris, 28; Louvre, Paris, 29; Private Collection/Index/© the estate of José Clemente Orozco, 30; British Library, London, 34; National Gallery, London, 35; Bury Art Gallery and Museum, 38; National Archaeological Museum, Athens, 40; Private Collection, 41; Private Collection, 42; Wilhelm Lehmbruck Museum, Duisberg, 43; Musée d'Orsay, Paris/Giraudon, 44.

Index